Start TO Finish
Second Series

FROM Seed TO Cattail

LISA OWINGS

LERNER PUBLICATIONS   Minneapolis

TABLE OF Contents

Lerner Publications Company
A division of Lerner Publishing Group, Inc.
241 First Avenue North
Minneapolis, MN 55401 USA

For reading levels and more information, look up this title at www.lernerbooks.com.

Library of Congress Cataloging-in-Publication Data

Names: Owings, Lisa, author.
Title: From seed to cattail / Lisa Owings.
Other titles: Start to finish (Minneapolis, Minn.). Second series.
Description: Minneapolis : Lerner Publications Company, [2017] | Series: Start to finish. Second series | Includes bibliographical references and index.
Identifiers: LCCN 2016037279 (print) | LCCN 2016038339 (ebook) | ISBN 9781512434439 (lb : alk. paper) | ISBN 9781512450958 (eb pdf)
Subjects: LCSH: Typha—Life cycles—Juvenile literature.
Classification: LCC QK495.T9 O95 2017 (print) | LCC QK495.T9 (ebook) | DDC 584/.68—dc23

LC record available at https://lccn.loc.gov/2016037279

Manufactured in the United States of America
1-42092-25386-10/20/2016

Cattails are wetland plants. How do they grow?

Wind spreads a cattail's seeds.

In the fall, the bobbing brown head of a cattail bursts open. It soon grows shaggy with cottony fluff. This fluff contains the plant's seeds. They easily float away in the wind.

The cattail seeds begin to grow.

Cattail seeds **germinate** in the spring. A cattail
seed grows best in wet soil or shallow water. If it lands
somewhere moist enough, it sprouts in the spring.

A seed sends out shoots and roots.

A cattail seed sends its first set of leaves up toward the sun. In the ground, a stem called a **rhizome** creeps sideways. Roots branch off from the rhizome to gather nutrients.

Next, the cattail grows more leaves.

The plant grows more sets of long, narrow leaves. They stand almost upright. The leaves help collect air for the roots. They also store water.

The plant grows very tall.

A cattail can grow up to 10 feet (3 meters) tall! It reaches toward the sun. The sunlight helps it grow. Its long, strong leaves can be woven into mats and baskets.

It sends out more shoots underground.

In summer, cattail rhizomes make more shoots. These will become new cattail plants. In this way, cattails can spread quickly.

Then its flowers bloom.

In midsummer, long spikes bloom at the tops of the cattails. These spikes are male flowers. They are heavy with yellow **pollen**. Below them is a cluster of female flowers.

The flowers pollinate themselves.

The male flowers release their pollen onto the female flowers. Wind and insects also carry pollen between plants. After pollination, the male flowers drop away.

The cattail is ready to release its seeds.

By summer's end, the cattails look like corn dogs. The female flower cluster is brown and velvety. In fall, it splits open to expose its fluffy seeds. New cattails will grow the next spring!

Glossary

germinate: begin to grow

pollen: the fine yellow dust that allows plants to produce seeds

pollinate: to place pollen on a plant so it can form seeds

rhizome: a thick stem that grows horizontally in the ground and puts out shoots and roots

shoots: parts of new plants that are just starting to grow

Further Information

Bullard, Lisa. *The Everglades*. Minneapolis: Lerner Publications, 2010. Read about one of America's most famous wetland regions.

Indiana DNR: Cattails
http://www.in.gov/dnr/kids/5846.htm
Learn more about the cattail's many uses on this site.

Minnesota DNR: Cattail
http://dnr.state.mn.us/minnaqua/speciesprofile/cattail.html
Check out detailed pictures and descriptions of the cattail.

Rose, Caroline Starr. *Over in the Wetlands: A Hurricane-on-the-Bayou Story*. New York: Schwartz & Wade, 2015. A wetland ecosystem prepares for a hurricane in this illustrated story.

Yasuda, Anita. *Explore Native American Cultures!* White River Junction, VT: Nomad, 2013. Did you know American Indians used cattails to weave baskets and other items? Explore American Indian culture through crafts.

Index

Photo Acknowledgments

The images in this book are used with the permission of: © Glacyer/Dreamstime.com, p. 1; © Marek Kosmal/Dreamstime.com, p. 3; © Biosphoto/SuperStock, p. 5; © Zach Welty//Flickr (CC BY-SA 2.0), p. 7; © Bill Beatty/Visuals Unlimited, Inc., p. 9; © Imagic Elements/Alamy, p. 11; © Noppharat_th/Deposit Photos, p. 13; © iStockphoto.com/Baxternator, p. 15; © Darlyne A. Murawski/Getty Images, p. 17; © Brais Seara/Getty Images, p. 19; © Eric Vondy/Getty Images, p. 21.

Cover: © Robert Asento/Shutterstock.com.

Main body text set in Arta Std Book 20/26. Typeface provided by International Typeface Corp.

LERNER
e
SOURCE

Expand learning beyond the printed book. Download free, complementary educational resources for this book from our website, www.lerneresource.com.